I0117979

THE SOUND
OF WATER

A Psychology of the Soul

JOSHUA K. LINDEN

**TURNING
STONE
PRESS**

First published in 2014 by
Turning Stone Press, an imprint of
Red Wheel/Weiser, LLC
With offices at:
665 Third Street, Suite 400
San Francisco, CA 94107
www.redwheelweiser.com

Copyright © 2014 by Joshua K. Linden

All rights reserved. No part of this publication may be
reproduced or transmitted in any form or by any means,
electronic or mechanical, including photocopying,
recording, or by any information storage and retrieval
system, without permission in writing from Red Wheel/
Weiser, LLC. Reviewers may quote brief passages.

ISBN: 978-1-6852-088-3

Cover design by Jim Warner
Cover image: © iBird/Shutterstock

Printed in the United States of America
10 9 8 7 6 5 4 3 2 1

In fond memory of
Father Ralph Hamlet

CONTENTS

ACKNOWLEDGMENTS

To my wife Liz for her steadfast love and support and to Reed, Richard, and numerous other friends and colleagues with whom countless hours of discussion led to writing *The Sound of Water*. Lastly, to the Red Wheel/Weiser editorial team that put so much time and care into making *The Sound of Water* a reality.

AUTHOR'S INTRODUCTORY NOTES TO THE READER

The Sound of Water is meant to be an art form — not a science. Most of what is written in this book can be neither proven nor disproven except through one's personal experience.

The Sound of Water draws from psychology, philosophy, and religion. Some might say it also draws from spirituality. However, in *The Sound of Water*, spirit is understood as that which unifies love and truth. In-depth explanations and examples are kept to a minimum; leaving them to each reader's body of knowledge and creative imagination. Whether the reader agrees or disagrees with any statements in *The Sound of Water* is less important to the author than the discussion the statements generate. Lastly, although *The Sound of Water* is loosely grounded in Christian theology, it is the hope of the author that what is discussed is equally applicable and easily translatable to any major religion's core teachings.

DIAGRAM OF A COMMON HUMAN EXPERIENCE

Hopefully the following diagram will be useful in assisting the reader in understanding the relationships of subjects discussed in *The Sound of Water* — keeping in mind that nothing of any individual's being remains static.

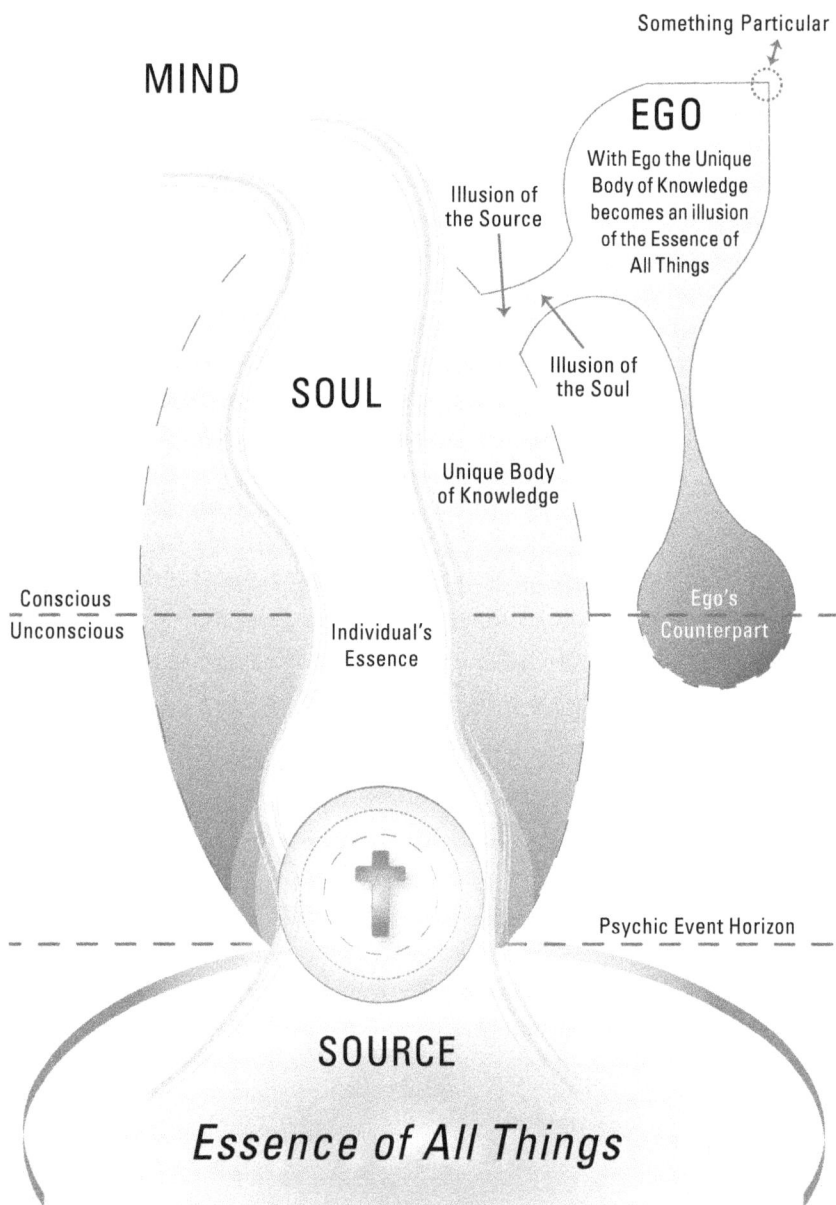

Something Particular

MIND

EGO

With Ego the Unique Body of Knowledge becomes an illusion of the Essence of All Things

Illusion of the Source

SOUL

Illusion of the Soul

Unique Body of Knowledge

Conscious
Unconscious

Individual's Essence

Ego's Counterpart

Psychic Event Horizon

SOURCE

Essence of All Things

The Hunt

I am moving silently through the jungle. I am my tribe's most recognized warrior sent to track down the *Midnight Priest*[1] and destroy him. He has been terrorizing the children in our village for countless moons and we the elders are determined to stop his intrusions into the peace and welfare of our people.

This is the jungle and in the jungle it is only jungle law that rules — kill or be killed. The *Midnight Priest* knows this and is in flight for his life — knowing that I, *Turtle Wolf*, am hunting him. He knows that I am of the *Great Soul* over whom he has no power.

I am called *Turtle Wolf* because I have the patience of the turtle and the hunting skills of the wolf.

I am the perfect hunter — hunting a very bewildered and confused beast. *The Midnight Priest* does not have the capacity to comprehend those of us over whom he has no power — no means with which to frighten.

He is near. I inhale deeply through my nostrils — enjoying the sweet fragrance of his terror. He knows that he and his fairy tale time have come to an end.

INTRODUCTION

There was a Great Man whose followers had left Him to go into town to buy some food. He walked to a village well where there was a woman who was considered to be an outcast. He asked the woman, "Will you give me a drink of water?"

The woman replied, "You are a great and respected man, and I am a social outcast. How is it that you would receive a drink from me?"

The great man replied, "If you knew the gift of God and who it is that asks you for a drink, you would have asked him and he would have given you living water."

"Sir," the woman said, "you have nothing to draw with and the well is deep. Where can you get this living water? Are you greater than our father who gave us the well and drank from it himself, as did also his sons and his livestock?"

He replied, "Everyone who drinks this water will be thirsty again, but whoever drinks the water I give them will never thirst. Indeed, the water I give them will become in them a spring of water welling up to eternal life."[2]

ONE

I do not, nor cannot speak for God.

Whatever God is, is beyond my purview.

There are some who presume to speak for God. For instance, they may say, "God expects...God wants...God feels...God thinks..." But the God about which they speak, is their ego "...I expect...I want...I feel...I think."[3]

Never confuse *ego* and God. There are many who do, and their confusion causes many problems for themselves as well as others.

Your studies and experience will teach you whether or not to believe in the existence of God.

My studies and experience have taught me that God does exist. This is a good thing, which I hope that in (this) the word, these sentences, this book, you will be compelled to go further in your studies and experience concerning questions of God.

For the purpose of *Sound of Water*, God is *through human perception* a form or aspect of Infinite Perfection. This aspect can be thought of and considered to exist in many forms such as, but not exclusively — love, beauty, truth, and scientific certainty. In *Sound of Water* this aspect or form of God is written about and understood to be the First Person of the Christian Trinity — the *Heavenly Father*.

TWO

nderlying the words in this book is essence. This essence is the same that exists when one looks out at a natural landscape and recognizes a wholeness or oneness. This essence permeates the trees, the fields, the clouds, the streams, the creatures — all that is. It is also the essence of each of us before knowledge and human consciousness. It is the essence of creation.

This essence is who each of us are when first born. It exists before anyone teaches us that we are something other than the essence of creation.

The words written here, and their essence, are what your Mind is aware of in this moment.

When the essence of all things is conscious of itself in one's being, one experiences the *Source*.[4]

The Sound of Water is meant to point you in the direction of this Source. This is where your essence and the essence of all things flow into one another — without deception, distortion, or corruption.

THREE

Music, art and knowledge potentially awaken one to the existence of the Source. Many spiritual writings point towards the Source. A great enlightened teacher's life can awaken one to the Source. There are many ways in which awakening to the Source can occur.

Your Mind has a relationship to the Source. A relationship is a form. The form or relationship of one's Mind and the Source is the Soul.[5]

It is a very important form that requires daily recollection, maintenance, and meditation if it is to remain in a state of Pure *Soul*—without deception, distortion, or corruption.

FOUR

Years of living and its formation of memories often cause one to forget the real Source as well as the form of the Soul.

Sometimes one comes to believe that another is the Source. Sometimes one tries to possess the Source and claim it for oneself.[6] Sometimes a culture elevates a dream, goal, or value as being the Source. Oftentimes these illusions of the Source are so tempting that one comes to believe that they are greater than the true and real Source.

When one becomes convinced of an unreal, make-believe Source, the Soul becomes distorted, corrupted, and diseased—one begins living an untruth and an unreality.

Untruths establish separation, duality, and suffering. However, the essence that is of all things, united and flowing into one's essence, creating the Source, exists without separation—without deception, distortion, or corruption.

The Mind recognizes and experiences the real Source through the alleviation of psychological and emotional suffering.

FIVE

A Soul is distorted when one knows the Source through someone or something that is external to oneself. These paths to the Source are indirect, socially constructed, and potentially dangerous.

When one's Mind is indirectly and externally connected with the Source, one is subject to socially generated guilt, fear, and doubt.

Although a masterpiece or a guru may awaken one's Mind to the Source, a true awakening does not result from dependence on the masterpiece or guru.

A true awakening occurs when one's Soul finds itself at peace and alive — existing without guilt, fear, or doubt. This state of being exists when the Mind experiences the Source: the essence of all things and one's essence flowing through one's Soul.

The Soul is at rest when personal and universal essence is not dependent on anyone or anything in particular.[7] When there is dependence on someone or something particular, *ego* is created.[8]

Egos always create separation and distortion of creation and reality; whereas the Source is always experienced as the union of creation and reality.

SIX

Most individuals are able to maintain a semblance of a healthy ego by associating their ego with a productive collective endeavor. However, because the ego creates separation, one normally lives a life of some inner and outer conflict as long as the ego exists.

Society's structures and laws are established in part to prevent unhealthy egos from fertilizing, taking root, and growing. When unhealthy egos are allowed to thrive, pain, suffering, and chaos often result.

Transcending social reality into a state of conscious reality happens when one awakens and comprehends: *I am not anything or anyone I have ever believed that I am.*

When one lets go of all sociologically assigned labels, descriptions, and values, one becomes simply one's consciousness, existing without containment in the realization of enlightenment.

SEVEN

T
hree *states of Mind* can occur when the Soul is
troubled: loneliness, boredom, and depression.
In these states the Soul is conveying to the
Mind that something is missing in order for the Mind and
the Source to be united. That which seems to be missing is
a result of a barrier or boundary the ego has constructed.
This construct is an illusion that creates an indirect path
to the Source resulting in a troubled state of the Mind.

The real essence that flows from these words into your
Mind, and your Mind that flows into *the meaning* of these
words is the Source — the words themselves written in this
book are not the Source as they are indirect.[9]

This Source exists whether you are worshipping in a
church or temple, having dinner with family and friends,
taking a walk, or sitting silently by a river.

This Source, the experience of the essence of all things
conscious within you, is not dependent on this book, nor
anything, or anyone else in particular.

Nothing is missing when you are experiencing the
Source.

EIGHT

An ego is established through an indirect and disconnected path to the Source. Just as many mistake their ego for God, so too do many mistake their ego's connection with their body of knowledge for the Source.

The connection, through which one is deluded into believing that it is the Source, is the ego's explanation and defense. As such this illusion is the ego's justification for its existence.

When one releases this connection between the ego and one's body of knowledge, and reawakens to the Soul as the direct path with the Source, the Mind quiets in its natural real Mind-Source form or relationship that is the Soul.

Freedom from indirect paths to the Source allows the Mind to merge and become one with the Source — to exist without the separation and the suffering that the ego creates.

NINE

The Source may or may not be God. Like superposition in quantum physics the Source may exist simultaneously in both states.

I am unable to say. However, I am able to say that it is impossible for anyone to possess the Source — it is only possible for one to experience the Source.

It is more than likely that the Source *belongs* to God.[10]

The Source is the well-spring from which creation occurs. The stars and the planets, life and culture originate from the Source.

Inspired literature, art, music, and scientific discovery originate from the Source.

You and I originate from the Source.

TEN

I t may be said that the Source is the present and that
it is experienced in the present.

The present is everything that is. It is actual
and real.

One is conscious of the present through experiencing and knowing. Likewise one is conscious of the Source
through experiencing and knowing. When the path
between the Mind and the Source is direct and uncor-
rupted through the Soul, such that the Mind merges
with the Source, experiencing and knowing also merge,
becoming one and the same thing.

When this happens, the Mind enters into reality
and the Soul enters into what may be described as a state
of divinity.[11]

ELEVEN

The present is the only actual reality. It is where, through the Source, creation is always occurring.[12] The past and future are states of unreality that one constructs. They can be altered in endless ways depending on the particulars one chooses to include in the unreality.

Living for the past or living for the future is living for something that does not exist. Existence only happens in the present and is the essence of all things that flow through the Source.

Unrealities always return to the reality and truth of the present. The Soul cannot tolerate for long periods of time the distortions that are made in the attempt to maintain a belief that an unreality is real. The Soul is at peace when the Mind and the Source are one in and of the present.

TWELVE

The basic form of all unrealities is not-present.

One creates or imagines an unreality; either in a past-present form or a present-future form, when one believes something particular is missing from actual existence or the present. When one conjures up an unreality, the Mind is temporarily separated from the Source, and in this process the Soul suffers.

This process of temporarily separating from the Source is a normal human activity that facilitates learning — the accumulation of knowledge. What is abnormal or inhuman is when one gives a mental permanence to the unreality and begins to lose sight of and the ability to return to reality and thereby the Source.

Individuals who lose the ability to return their Minds to the Source, to reconnect with the Source, are often referred to as *lost Souls*.

THIRTEEN

Every individual's body of knowledge is unique —
comprised of different experiences, studies, memories, and perception. As such, every individual's
experience and awareness of the Source is different and
unique.

A normal human experience of the Source is an individual's Mind being drawn toward the Source, fulfilling
a natural state of one's essence united with the essence
of all things. This natural state becomes corrupted when
one connects to something particular that is socially constructed and external to one's own being. This is a basic
form of *missing* and establishes a basic process of *searching* — a movement from reality into unreality in search of
the particular that one believes to be important.

This process of searching begins with one imagining
an unreality, a not-present form in which the Source is
believed to be reflected or contained in something particular that is socially constructed and external to one's being.

A healthy example of this process is when an individual hears a beautiful sound that causes the Soul to have
a similar experience as when the Mind and Source are

one. The individual may search for the instrument that produces this particular sound and imagines an unreality of owning and playing the instrument. If the unreality becomes a reality and the individual acquires the instrument, and diligently practices, the Source within the individual will be expressed directly when one is playing the instrument — the sound of the Source will manifest itself in reality. The individual will have become a musician who is said to *have Soul*.[13]

FOURTEEN

W hat one is doing and experiencing at any given moment in time is reality.

What one imagines or thinks one did in the past, or will do in the future, or what one is doing in the present in any form other than what is actually occurring are all unrealities.

Unrealities are useful in many ways. A primary way that an unreality is useful is that it teaches what reality is by awakening one to what it is not.

Often unrealities can be dangerous and even destructive. This happens when one believes that the unreality is actually real. Because the Source does not exist in any unreality, believing that the unreality is reality disconnects one from the Source.

One of the greatest dangers occurs when belief in the unreality is so strong that one actively sets out to convince others that the unreality or illusion is real. Dysfunctional families are often formed around such illusions. Many destructive cults have temporarily existed as a result of a collective belief in such illusions. Entire nations have collapsed as a result of such illusions. This was true in the nationalist sentiments in Germany, Italy, and Japan during WWII.

It is important for an individual to be aware when contemplating an unreality. After the lessons of the unreality are learned, it is important that one have the ability to return the Mind back to reality and thereby the Source from which life, truth, and peace originate and exist.

FIFTEEN

One of the greatest uses of unrealities exists in the form of *what might be*.

However, this is a form in which potential violence exists. It is also a form in which potential resolution to conflict exists.

When people who believe in unrealities go to such an extreme that they are willing to attempt to suppress or even kill the Source, the result is always violence and suffering. When people allow the Source to manifest itself, the result is always resolution and peace.

Because the Source is the essence of all things, and always exists in the present and therefore what is real, its suppression or death is never permanently possible.

The Source will eventually manifest itself in all ways that are conceivable, as well as in ways far beyond the conception and imagination that are possible given the restrictions and limitations of knowledge in any given human era.

SIXTEEN

(Socrates) recognized that insight into one's own ignorance is the beginning of all knowledge.[14]

Most individuals spend a number of years living an unreality in which they are disconnected or distanced from the Source. As such they relate to things particular and not the Source. Believing in and sometimes even worshipping something other than the creator of the Source is fundamentally constructing one's belief structure or system around an untruth or self-deception.

There are two characteristics that are common to the core of an individual's unreality — denial of ignorance and assumption of oneself as *the* authority.

Living in an unreality is living in a world comprised of conclusions stemming from untruths and self-deceptions. As such the atmosphere or environment of knowledge based in unreality is an atmosphere or environment of egoistic illusion.

One begins to live again when one fully recognizes one's fundamental ignorance. In this process one releases an ego's false conclusions and re-establishes a right relationship with the Source that is united with Mind through the Soul. This is the beginning of real knowledge and truth.

SEVENTEEN

When a body of knowledge is structured around untruths and self-deceptions and one fully believes they are true, one of two things happens. Either the ego attempts to reject the existence of the Source, or the ego attempts to claim the Source for itself. Neither is entirely possible. Both attempts result in the suffering of one's Soul. The suffering increases as the intensity of rejection or possession of the Source increases.

Rejection of the Source is always injurious to the Soul. It causes the Soul, deprived of the well-spring of life, to wither like a plant that is deprived of water. Meanwhile, external to the individual's suffering, the Source never stops revealing itself in nature and through those who are conscious of its sacred existence.

Attempting to possess and own the Source is equally as dangerous and is also a potentially destructive psychology. The Source is infinitely more omnipresent than any individual's body of knowledge. What an ego claims to be as the Source is an illusion grounded in something particular that one believes one has and others do not.

When one ceases to deny or possess the Source, the Soul blossoms and the Mind expands. In this process of letting go, the Source begins again to express itself naturally in one's life.

However, if one does not cease to deny or possess the Source, the ego will become more rigid, and one's illusion of the Source will become more distorted — eventually resulting in increased personal and social damage.

It is especially important for young people to learn that individuals who deny the existence of the Source, as well as those who claim or imply to possess the Source are frequently disturbed and mentally unhealthy individuals. If one believes in the denial or possession of the Source by another, this can often lead to the denial or possession of the Source in oneself. However, this is not the same as atheism, which commonly interprets the Source as humanism.

Recognizing the Source in oneself, through one's essence, is simultaneously a recognition and acknowledgement of the essence of all things.

EIGHTEEN

A common way in which many unrealities begin is when one believes that a title is more important than the actual activity that leads to a title.

When playing music, writing, or solving equations is not a joyful, fascinating, passionate, and inspired activity — is not an activity of the Source manifesting itself in reality, the titles *musician, writer,* or *mathematician* are then without real meaning.

When a title is more important than the activity that leads to a title, one's ego becomes attached to a title's indirect particular associations. This form of pursuit is an ego imagining an unreality of what life will be like when a title is eventually received. When the title is finally attained, one is left with an activity devoid of a sense of personal meaning and purpose.[15]

Possessing a title and not the Soul of the title's activity leads to suffering.

Activities that are of the Source resonating in one's Soul lead to a lifetime of fulfillment. They contribute to the greater whole — being a part of the essence of all things.

Temptation of a title is an original sin — alienation from the Source, the well-spring of life.

NINETEEN

Cultures began to form thousands of years ago in many places. A culture is fundamentally a core of common agreements known as a belief system. In every culture, whether large or small, these agreements or beliefs pertain to almost everything having to do with existence and existing with one another in harmony.

Culture is organic—constantly growing, fluctuating, and changing depending on a myriad of factors, not the least of which is the merging of two or more distinct cultures.

Disagreements between distinct cultures cause negotiations or conflicts with the intention of arriving at common agreement.

Individuals are born into cultures, the collection of common agreements of which they had no part in forming.

An agreement is formed either in relationship to the Source or to something particular. Like an individual, the extent to which agreements are made in relationship to the Source, is the extent to which a culture is real and healthy. The extent to which the agreements are made in relationship to something particular is the extent to which a culture is unreal and unhealthy.

You and I were born into a culture in which we had no say as to its reality or unreality, health or lack of health. You and I were not present to either agree or disagree with our culture's belief system. It was created deep within the past of our ancestors — most of whom have long been forgotten.

TWENTY

One's ego is culturally constructed beginning with one's name. The ego attaches one's perception to the external world and begins the process of forming consciousness and unconsciousness. In this process most cultures usurp the Source — they make claim to being the essence of all things.

A fundamental universal form of the Source is friendship.

A culture that has usurped the Source defines *who* is a friend and *who* is not a friend, and *when* someone is a friend and *when* someone is not a friend.

Early in the formation of one's ego, when the Mind is still directly connected with the Source, one's experiences are feelings of *friendship* and sensations of joy.

As one grows, and the ego attaches itself to more and more particulars, one becomes increasingly conscious of the external as defined by culture and increasingly unconscious[16] of the Source. During this process the ego becomes increasingly differentiated between an understanding of friend that is of the ego and an understanding of not-friend that is the counterpart of the ego.[17]

During this period of mental growth it is important for individuals to have in their environments reminders of the Source.[18] Without reminders one frequently becomes increasingly unconscious of the existence of the Source.

TWENTY ONE

The ego is a necessary and important unreality. It is the means by which the essence of all things awakens and becomes conscious of itself in one's being.

The fundamental unreality of the ego is that as it grows and individuates, it comes to believe that it is the essence of the Mind. When full individuation occurs, the ego disintegrates — freeing the Mind to merge with the Source through the Soul.[19] When this happens, friendship returns to its rightful form as an essence of all things.

In this state of awakening one experiences a peace and joy that is often referred to as a heavenly bliss.

TWENTY TWO

In a state of awakening, when the ego disintegrates or ceases to exist, several important things happen.

As the ego is the way one relates to culture, when the ego ends or ceases to exist, one never-the-less continues to live in a culture, but does not necessarily relate to the culture. The Mind becomes one with the Source and not the culture's collective body of conclusions.

Egos have principal authorities that facilitate creation and growth. When the ego no longer exists, the principal authorities cease having power.

As the Mind rightfully reconnects with the Source, which is in everything and everywhere, *presence* and existing in the *present,* the Soul becomes magnified and intensified as it begins to re-experience the essence of all things. Simultaneously increased illumination occurs — a brighter emanation of the essence in all of nature.

An awakened Soul experiences a conscious oneness in and with everything and everyone, as the Source is always experienced without separation of any kind.

TWENTY THREE

When the ego disintegrates, an echo of the ego sometimes continues to exist. This echo is important for one's functioning in society. In a sense, it is an illusion that permits something with which others can relate — if even just in a name or an image. The echo of an ego, as with a word, allows meaning to exist in a conscious state.

The echo is like a tree that is perceived, thus allowing one to speak of it as a "tree." But the real relationship, the meaning, of the echo or the "tree" is through the Source — the essence that is of the person or the tree.

However, unlike a person or a tree, the echo of an ego is ultimately an unreality — without a connection to the Source other than a body of knowledge that perceives it.

TWENTY FOUR

A body of knowledge serves many purposes, not the least of which is to translate and interpret information, as well as to solve problems.

A body of knowledge serves an ego, and also by design translates and interprets with respect to the ego's prescribed dimensions. The ego looks for problems, real and imaginary, whose solutions one believes will support and strengthen it.

As a body of knowledge is primarily formed through cultural conditioning and the ego is one's connection with the culture, translations, interpretations, and solutions tend to be grounded in the body of the established cultural conclusions, regardless of the general health of the culture.

The less a culture is formed from the Source the unhealthier most egos in the culture become. Conversely, the more a culture is formed from the Source the healthier most egos in the culture become.

In either an unhealthy or healthy culture the end of individuation leads to the disintegration of the ego resulting in the healing of the Soul and the Source re-establishing its direct relationship with the Mind. The Soul's longing is always for the Source's direct expression—without the ego's distorted translations, interpretations, and solutions. The Soul thrives through the clear expression of the Source.

TWENTY FIVE

The ego tends to interact with the world through problems, real and imaginary. Egos thrive by relating to each other through commonly agreed upon conclusions.

Conclusions that are grounded in the Source create healthy relationships. Conclusions that have the sole purpose of strengthening egos frequently cause unhealthy relationships that oftentimes lead to conflict.

Conclusions and truths are not necessarily the same. Conclusions are primarily of the ego — truths are of consciousness and the Mind.

The Source exists with or without ego. However, an ego distorts the expression of the Source; whereas without ego the Source's expression becomes one of clarity.

The greater one's body of knowledge, when the ego does not exist, the greater are the truths and the beauty that the Soul is able to reveal of the Source.

TWENTY SIX

As is friendship, love is also the essence of the Source. Most readers intuitively know this.

The most rational part of one's body of knowledge is that which is born of the Source. The rational part of one's being is one's understanding of love.

Love, like the essence of all things, is without boundaries.

Boundaries are a form of unreality that is created by the ego for both constructive and destructive purposes. Boundaries that are established in order to study and comprehend something are useful and constructive. Boundaries that are established in order to possess something are destructive and have the potential to cause conflict and violence.

Attempting to possess love is not only impossible, but in the process of doing so one diminishes and eventually extinguishes the experience of love.

As love is the essence of all things, its experience is the experience of love flowing freely through everything and everyone.

TWENTY SEVEN

As the Source is the essence of all things flowing into the essence of one's being, and this essence is love, the reality of love is that it exists instantaneously in everything — including oneself. Most cultures teach contrary to this truth. They teach love one but not the other, or love those but not oneself. Ultimately in the process of individuation and the subsequent disintegration of the ego these teachings are comprehended as unreal.

The Mind united with the Source through one's Soul occurs within one's being — one's existence. Love flows through the Source into the Mind and returns to the Source that flows into all things, in the process manifesting as love in the world. This is the process of a Soul that is awakened. It is the experience of grace. It is the process that occurs in loving oneself while simultaneously, without possibility of doing otherwise, loving without separation or distinction.

One can witness this process in all the great works of art, literature, music, religions, and scientific discoveries — as well as in a neighbor's smile or a stranger's handshake.

TWENTY EIGHT

In loving yourself, consider what Jesus said: *Truly I tell you, unless you change and become like little children, you will never enter the kingdom of heaven.*[20]

There is an important aspect or feature of the Mind that experiences with neither the unreality of the past nor the unreality of the future. This is what one experiences when living entirely in the present — without condition, preconception, or intellectual judgment.

One recognizes and is simultaneously recognized. One interacts without separation between the internal and external worlds. One is known only in the immediate expression of the Source that is occurring. In this state one exists without cultural imprints, attributes, qualities, or characteristics — one experiences without ego. This is how a child experiences the world — free from the burden of living with expectation or preconception and therefore without alienation.

In this state there are no culturally predetermined reasons to prevent love, or the essence of all things from flowing freely in everyone and everything.

This is the verb of love, which is the only way a child knows love.

This is also the experience of pure consciousness.

TWENTY NINE

The opposite of a state of love is a state of extreme grandiosity. It is the experience of complete unconsciousness in which the body of knowledge is mistaken entirely for the essence of all things.

As one detaches from the Source, the ego and the ego's attachments to the body of knowledge grow. These are the irrational attachments.

As the relationship or form between the Mind and the ego increases, the health of the Soul diminishes. This is the opposite state of the natural and healthy form that exists when the Mind and the Source are connected and one through the Soul — unimpeded by the ego.

Although a Soul's functioning may become diminished and even seem to become non-existent, there always remains at least one attachment of the Mind to the Source through the Soul. This is what is commonly referred to as *saving grace*.

The ego attempts in many different ways to claim the Mind and the Source as its own — this never occurs in reality.

The experience of love is always greater than the experience of ego. Love cannot be contained.

THIRTY

Although most cultures imply otherwise, it is not possible to own the Mind.

The Mind can be nurtured, expanded, and protected — *it cannot be owned.* The Mind serves only the Source as the Source only serves the Mind. As such, when one acknowledges and honors the Source, the Mind becomes a servant that will assist one in discovering endless revelations about friendship, love, truth, and divinity that continuously flow from the Source.

An ego that attempts to own the Mind only ends up possessing a very limited body of knowledge. Just as with the Source, the Mind has no boundaries and therefore no form of containment.

The Mind is the consciousness of the Source. It provides one with the state of knowing.

The ego provides one with a state of thinking — which is restricted or contained to one's body of knowledge.

The Source is the light that illuminates both knowledge and knowing. The Mind is drawn to the light that illuminates truth.

The ego is drawn towards the light *and* the darkness, but does not have a rational capability to distinguish between the two.

The ego is capable of seeing truth where truth does not exist.

THIRTY ONE

The Mind is not a single body of knowledge. A Mind is born of collective bodies of knowledge, based in experience and studies that unite truths emanating from and revealing the Source. The Mind is expansive and without limit.

Humanity's identification and relationship to the Mind continuously grows. It is like a tree of eternal life growing from the Source. The existence of intelligence, wisdom, and compassion all serve the expansion of human understanding. Combined, they comprise the state of knowing.

The Mind is not who a person is.

One is the experience of Soul—the Mind and Source in union. One is the experience of cause and effect and perception refined in consciousness.

One is the experience of Mind—existing as a sense of oneself.

Potentially one is the experience of the essence of all things conscious of itself in one's being.

THIRTY TWO

O ne's body of knowledge born of experience and studies is important. It is a configuration of memory that allows one to answer such questions as *who*, *what*, *when*, *where*, and *how* — but not necessarily *why*.

Bodies of knowledge are structures of codes that have been broken — some correctly, and others incorrectly. Egos more often than not decode one's experience of the world incorrectly. They too often decipher the Mind or the Source as "I."

As many egos grow, they eventually attempt to decipher what is not given to be known. In so doing they often create unrealities. These unrealities are projections of the known into the unknown. Sometimes this results in exploration and other times this results in imagined beliefs whose intended purpose is to sustain the ego.

Imagined beliefs that can neither be substantiated nor unsubstantiated are catalysts that often lead to the disintegration of the ego.

Arguments based in the ego and not the Mind never stand up to the test of time.

THIRTY THREE

K nowledge that is of the Source is extremely valuable and timeless. Knowledge that is not of the Source may be temporarily instructive or useful, but by its very nature is unreal and temporal.

When the ego disintegrates, one's body of knowledge is refined, rounded, and smoothed in a way that results in wholeness and interconnectedness — much like a weathered river stone. Corruptions, deceptions, untruths, and illusions disintegrate with the ego. One's body of knowledge increasingly replicates and mirrors a larger form of the Soul.

In this form the Mind is able to envision universal beauty and truth — two of the most basic elements of the Source.

When the ego disintegrates, its authority loses its meaning and purpose. At the same time the chaos and confusion of the world loses its meaning and purpose.

One understands that the Source is neither without meaning, nor does it ever exist in a state of disorder.

One is drawn towards the light of beauty and truth — the Mind attracted towards a natural order in the essence of all things.

THIRTY FOUR

An ego draws from a body of knowledge and points to something particular saying, "You (or this or those) are the reason *the good* is not happening. *That* is the cause of my suffering. Eliminate *that* and *the good* will happen and my suffering will end."

It has been said, *never appease a tyrant.*

The ego has the potential of becoming the ultimate tyrant.

The ego is fundamentally not concerned with the welfare of others. It is not truly conscious of others.

An ego frequently uses its body of knowledge to create the illusion, or deception of caring, concern, and compassion. In this behavior the ego can, in some cases, be very subtle. It has the capability of masking itself with expressed concern for others that it does not actually feel.

Empathy is of the Source — not the ego.

In a state of being completely possessed by one's ego, an individual becomes unconscious of the Mind — mistaking one's body of knowledge for the Mind.

When one arrives at this state in which concern for others is nothing more than an unreality, disintegration of the ego is likely.

When the ego says, *this is who I am — this body of knowledge* exclusive of others, the ego can become overwhelmed by the reality of the truth that one's knowledge is almost entirely comprised of other's lives and teachings. One's body of knowledge is, in fact, almost entirely the knowledge that others shared rather than claimed or possessed as their own.

This process or experience of an ego's disintegration and one's awakening is commonly referred to as *The Dark Night of the Soul*.[21]

INTERLUDE

The Present

After the Midnight Priest's demise or departure, I, Turtle Wolf, burned his body according to his tribe's sacraments, gathered his ashes, and then walked for nearly a full cycle of the moon through fields and forests, returning his ashes to his village the people called the Time Travelers.

As I approached the ring of huts and thatch houses, a young girl came out along the path to greet me. She introduced herself as Morning Star. This was their custom — to greet strangers with the friendliest of faces.

After we had greeted one another, she took my hand and led me down into the center of the village where we were met by the tribe's most distinguished hunter, who the girl introduced as Great Eagle. This, too, was one of their customs — a statement making clear to strangers that they were a strong, protected, and safe people.

Great Eagle asked me the purpose of my being there. I explained what I was returning and handed him the leather pouch containing the Midnight Priest's ashes.

He turned and kneeled next to the young girl, whispered something to her as he handed her the pouch, where

upon she ran off towards the far end of the village and dis-
appeared into a hut.

Great Eagle, asked me to follow him, and led me to a
stream with a waterfall next to the village.

There, after bathing, I sat quietly on a fallen log and
meditated on the soothing roar of the waterfall.

At dusk, the young girl and Great Eagle came and led
me to an area where there was a great feast set out before
us. The village council headed by the village elder, the
Chief of Dreams, and I dined and conversed into the dark
of the night.

Then there was a ceremony of blessings, at the end of
which Great Eagle handed me a sheet of parchment with
writing on both sides. He explained that sometime ago he
had also hunted *his* village's Midnight Priest. As was happening now, that Midnight Priest's tribe had given him
this page of parchment.

The Chief of Dreams declared that because my people
were willing to end their fears, just as his people had once
expressed the same willingness, the page was now to be
entrusted to us.

That night I went to sleep and dreamt many dreams.
When I awoke everyone and everything of the village had
vanished—traveled away in time.

I gathered my belongings and set out on the journey
home; carrying with me the page of parchment I had been
given.

THIRTY FIVE

Fear, guilt, and doubt are not of and do not flow from the Source.

Like hunger or exhaustion, fear, guilt, and doubt are normal experiences when they relate to immediate circumstances. Fear, guilt, and doubt that emanate from an unreality of the past or future are often socially constructed. These are an ego's response to imagined unrealities.

Fear, guilt, and doubt flow from the part of one's body of knowledge having to do with belief structures — primarily those that have to do with culturally constructed values of good and evil, right and wrong, heaven and hell.

Only *the good* flows from the Source. Cultural values established in relationship to anything other than the Source are inherently mistaken and are causes of irrational fear, guilt, and doubt.

An ego that is aligned with incorrect cultural values inevitably distances one's awareness further from the Source. Distance from the Source causes a Soul to suffer.

When the Mind and Source are united, one understands incorrect belief structures for what they are: a wasteland into which one travels only with an abundant amount of water and supplies.[22]

THIRTY SIX

When one is born, one is awake to or conscious of the Source — the Mind and Source are not separated. As one grows one learns a culture's values and beliefs and in the process begins to be unconscious of this early state of consciousness. Developed egos frequently mistake this unconscious state for consciousness — which is actually the ego and its relationship with a body of knowledge.

It is for this reason that an individual can be very educated, and yet very unconscious.

An individual may be able to reference many bodies of knowledge, but if the person has no understanding of the Source from which all original and authentic knowledge is derived, then the individual does not experience a true state of knowing — which is consciousness — the Mind and Source flowing freely together in and through one's Soul.

Such an individual may have many thoughts, but will have little if any actual knowing.

THIRTY SEVEN

Intuition is a process of the Mind, a state of knowing, and the Source flowing freely between one another—unobstructed by an ego's psychological restrictions.

Psychological restrictions occur in the forms *I am allowed to be* or *I am not allowed to be*, *I should* or *I should not*, *I must* or *I must not*. One's response to these forms can seem like intuition but are actually forms of maintenance or growth of the ego.

Responses to psychological restrictions are in relationship to a comparative: better, smarter, quicker, or nicer, to name just a few. The goal of the response is a superlative: best, smartest, quickest, or nicest.

A musician may study music with a perspective of growing the ego. Likewise a musician may study music with the love that is experienced through the expression of the Source in the music. Either may result in the title *The Best*.

Joy for the former is contingent upon winning the title—which is this musician's purpose.

Joy for the latter is the beauty of the Source expressed through music. As was stated earlier, this musician is said *to have Soul*—the experience of the Mind and Source flowing freely from the music. This intuitive existential experience is the second musician's purpose.

THIRTY EIGHT

Inherent in egos are competitive structures or beliefs.
Inherent in the Source is love and beauty.

Love that flows from the Source, through the
Soul, and into the Mind, when free from an ego's competitive structures, develops intuition — a state of knowing.
One knows love and beauty without having to mentally
frame them within a structure.

An ego needs to think, analyze, contrast, calculate,
and judge love and beauty in relationship to psychological
restrictions created from cultural and egoistic constructs.
These processes of the ego are fundamentally forms of
competition.

Cultural constructs may or may not approximate
reality depending on the directness of their relationship
to the Source.

If an individual is unconscious of the Source, the individual is incapable of knowing love and beauty, except as
they are constructed by the culture.

An individual capable of intuition knows love and
beauty regardless of what a cultural construct states
they are.

Love and beauty, and the Source from which they emanate, and the Mind that is conscious of them, transcend every culture and precede every body of knowledge.

Love and beauty are a priori to human origin.

THIRTY NINE

There are countless levels of culture beginning with the broadest or most comprehensive: the global or human culture. This culture is fractured into national cultures that are fractured into local cultures that are fractured into religious, ethnic, and socio-economic cultures. All of these cultures influence the most important culture, the one that has the greatest impact on the creation of an individual's body of knowledge and ego-orientation — that of the *family culture*.

All cultures have reminders of the Source — some very primitive and others very evolved. They can be found in homes, churches, temples, synagogues, schools, and other public places. Reminders are in a culture's symbols, scriptures, artwork, literature, music, and sciences.

Nature is a constant reminder of the Source and because nature exists everywhere, reminders of the Source are always present or accessible.

Children are one of the greatest reminders of the Source.

Reminders of the Source are a society's greatest treasures.

The more reminders that a family acknowledges, experiences, and honors, the healthier a family is.

In every culture exceptional individuals occasionally appear who transcend a culture's reminders — who express the Source directly in the lives they live.[23]

FORTY

omes need reminders of the Source.

Typically a home is where children mature into adolescence and then become young adults. This is a time when one's body of knowledge is growing rapidly and at the same time the conscious and unconscious are being formed.

Reminders of the Source in a home become visual and verbal imprints in a young person's unconscious. They also can become a part of a young person's consciousness.

Reminders of the Source must never be oppressive. If they are oppressive they reflect a restrictive dogma of an ego and not the nature of the Source.

Carl Jung wrote: *The ultimate fate of every dogma is that it gradually becomes Soulless. Life wants to create new forms, and therefore, when a dogma loses its vitality, it must perforce activate the archetype that has always helped man to express the mystery of the Soul.*

Homes that have either oppressive reminders of the Source, or homes that have few, if any, reminders of the Source, are recipes for psychological problems and even potential tragedy.

In either case the unconscious becomes a world without memory of the Source, of near total darkness in which fear, guilt, and doubt thrive.

FORTY ONE

Most families have a member of the family that is the authority. Being an authority of a family is one of the most important responsibilities any individual can undertake.

The authority of a family must decide what reminders of the Source to include in the home. More importantly, the authority must be fully aware of that which the reminders point or refer to. Most importantly, the authority must have the humility and wisdom to never waver from the truth that the Source is infinitely greater than any individual living in or outside of the family.

One of the greatest reminders of the Source is an authority's Soulful guidance. Soulful guidance only occurs if it is given with the knowledge of the unique individual's Soul to whom it is directed.

If each member of a family spends an afternoon in an art museum, a day listening to classical music, and an hour in the garden, and are asked to choose a favorite painting, music piece, and flower, the chances are that each family member will choose differently.

Every individual's Soul is different — the Mind and Source form is different. A healthy family culture is one in which this truth is honored. Ego-orientations grow in relationship to each individual's unique experience of the Source or own Soul.

However, oftentimes an authority will insist that only the authority's chosen painting, musical composition, and flower are the correct choices. Family members become nothing more than extensions of the authority's ego.

It has been said many times, in many ways, by many individuals: *Truth is one — paths are many.*

A painting, musical piece, and a flower are specifics or particulars to each individual's process of individuation — what truly matters is the Source that is the One towards which the reminders point.

FORTY TWO

A family's authority chooses and establishes the core values of the family. Universal values such as *the way, the life and the truth* are of the Source and therefore not dependent on time and events.[24] Specific values such as winning a medal are of the ego and dependent on time and events.

An important core value is that the family authority has a named, spoken, and expressed higher authority. Without a named higher authority the family authority will be perceived as possessing the Source — which is a characteristic of the ego.

The body of knowledge of someone who is twenty-five is much greater than the body of knowledge of a five year-old child. Thus, when a family authority does not name and express a higher authority, the child can potentially develop the unconscious belief while growing into young adulthood that the family authority is something of a God. The result of this is that the family ceases to be a family and becomes a cult.

As an individual matures, a part of the individuation process is accepting or rejecting core values that have been expressed by the family's authority. When core values are universal, and there is a named and expressed higher authority, individuation ends in the balance and harmony of the Source. When a core value is specific and/or there is no named and expressed higher authority, individuation will frequently end in cognitive dissonance and dysfunction.

FORTY THREE

A functional or healthy family culture is one in which the member who is the family's authority not only points to a higher authority, but is also aware of the family as a whole—that each member's Soul has a distinct meaning and purpose to fulfill within the larger body of the family.

A family's authority also needs to appreciate and honor the larger body of humanity—that the individual family and the family of humanity are inter-related and interconnected. The family's authority needs to accept that individual members will someday need to transition into the larger culture—that members' egos need to relate to and serve the greater whole and the greater good than just the family.

Family members will someday need to shed the ego-orientation they established in the family and merge their perspective into the Mind that is of all being: the tree of wisdom and the Soul of all humanity.

A healthy family authority acknowledges this process and bows to the higher authority.

In doing so the family members are set free.

FORTY FOUR

When one matures and individuates to the point at which the ego ceases to exist, the universal culture of the human family and the essence of all things become one of the Mind. An individual becomes conscious that human evolution is the formation and expansion of Mind — the Source's consciousness of existence and the reality of itself.

The more that the Source, being conscious of itself as the essence of all things realizes itself in an individual, the more that an individual realizes beauty and truth. This process causes one to awaken or come alive.

> *Don't ask yourself what the world needs; ask yourself what makes you come alive. And then go do that — what the world needs is people who have come alive.*[25]

Awakening, or coming alive, is more difficult for some than others depending on the extent of attachments one has to the ego.

An ego-orientation is primarily concerned with appearance — how one looks compared to others — which gives people, objects, and actions their meaning.

However, even the most extreme psychopaths can exhibit outward appearances of being good.

One comes alive when the ego ceases and its sustaining preconditions and conclusions no longer restrict an individual's Mind—one knows beauty, truth, and the good not through appearance but in reality.

The experience of reality is living life awake.

FORTY FIVE

There are many ways for one to maintain a healthy Soul — a freely flowing relationship of the Mind with the Source. The most important and powerful way one does this is through a deep relationship with another person who experiences, knows, and honors the Source's creative and vital power.

When two or more actual experiences of the Source unite, there emerges a recognition that the experiences are of one and the same Source. This common experience causes the Mind to expand.

Bodies of knowledge grow, fluctuate, alter, diminish, and increase — moving in numerous directions depending on changing circumstances.

The direction of the Mind is always towards infinity, eternity, and wholeness.

This is one of many reasons for creation and existence in general, and the beginning and evolution of humans in particular — to expand the Mind that is fully conscious of the Source.

FORTY SIX

The Mind is universal. It reveals itself through and in universal laws. The following are just a few of these laws:

- All that one knows will never be revealed

- Fear is not good

- Biological adaptation does not move backwards

- Physical laws do not change

- Love has no boundaries

Many laws put forward by individuals and groups as universal pertain only to some people, some circumstances, and some periods of time — these are actually laws pertaining to a culture and ego. They are destined for extinction.

Universal laws are timeless. They exist whether or not humans are aware of them. They are known on any planet that has intelligent life capable of realizing them. They transcend time and place.

When you or any conscious being is free of ego, conscious of the Source and the essence of all things flowing into the Mind, through experience of the Soul, you will be conscious of the universal Mind, and you will know through your intuition the essence of all things becoming conscious of itself in your being.

You will know peace of Mind.

FORTY SEVEN

The creative arts, scientific discovery, and religious rituals in all their various forms lead to expansion of the Mind—not in the initial experience of observing, hearing, participating, or understanding, but rather in the later reflection that results in the revelation of truth.

Revelation occurs not within one's body of knowledge, but rather in awakening to that which is beyond one's body of knowledge. This is the field of mystery into which humans are compelled to explore.

Dragons are culturally created mythologies and belief systems that frighten individuals from exploration that reveals the Source.[26] Living solely for the purpose of serving a transient culture or society quiets the culture's dragons.

However, when one awakens to the energy of the Source and its universal form of the essence of all things, the dragons are transformed and can serve as structures that protect one's sacred relationship with the Soul—the sacred relationship between the Mind and the Source.

Dragons are meant to serve—not to be served.

FORTY EIGHT

As an adult, if one is bound to an ego, real freedom of choice is not possible — choices have
already been made by others — though one will
believe that they are free to make choices. This is one of
the deceptions of an ego.

On the other hand, if one is an adult without ego, one
lives life with the most amazing gift — which is referred to
as *free will* or *choice.*

The Source is not a master, nor is the Mind or a Soul a
master. You are the master. You are entirely free to choose
how the Source manifests itself in your life and in your
being — given your unique body of knowledge.

Fields of exploration are endless — infinite, eternal,
and whole. The only restrictions to one's exploration are
psychological and constrained by the ego.

Whatever and however you choose to express the
Source, if it is without psychological constraints of the
ego, it will be right, true, and beautiful — though a culture's dragons may attempt to convince you otherwise.

All the critics of Van Gogh and Galileo could not
negate the beauty and truth of what they revealed — the
energy and power in art and in thought.

FORTY NINE

Some readers may find the following quote to be helpful:

Unfortunately we find systems of education today which have departed so far from the plain Truth, that they now teach us to be proud of what we know and ashamed of ignorance. This is doubly corrupt. It is corrupt not only because pride is in itself a mortal sin, but also because to teach pride in knowledge is to put up an effective barrier against any advance upon what is already known, since it makes one ashamed to look beyond the bonds imposed by one's ignorance.

To any person prepared to enter with respect into the realm of his great and universal ignorance, the secrets of being will eventually unfold, and they will do so in a measure according to his freedom from natural and indoctrinated shame in his respect of their revelation.

In the face of the strong, and indeed violent, social pressures against it, few people have been prepared to take this simple and satisfying course towards sanity. And in a society where a prominent psychiatrist can advertise that, given the chance, he would have treated Newton to electric shock therapy, who can blame any person for being afraid to do so?

The quote continues:

And yet those with the courage to tread this path to real discovery are not only offered practically no guidance on how to do so, they are actively discouraged and have to set about it in secret, pretending meanwhile to be diligently engaged in the frantic diversions and to conform with the deadening personal opinions which are being continually thrust upon them.

In these circumstances, the discoveries that any person is able to undertake represent the places where, in the fact of induced psychosis, he has, by his own faltering and unaided efforts, returned to sanity.[27]

FIFTY

The Source that is absolute good, and the Mind that is also absolute good, and the Soul that unites the two is also absolute good. They are of God.

In this sense, no human being is evil, as a human being is fundamentally this union. However, every body of knowledge of every human being has a core of belief structures that form a psychology — both constructive and destructive.

Many psychologies may be said to be incarnations of evil. These psychologies are disinterested and unconcerned with the Source. They are psychological embodiments of cultural distortions, deceptions, and lies. They manifest themselves in ways that *result in suffering*. In this regard they are referred to as demons. Angels, on the other hand, are those that manifest in ways that result in the *alleviation of suffering*.

The death of Osama Bin Laden had nothing to do with vengeance; though some would say otherwise — it had everything to do with extinguishing his psychology.

Psychologies, both good and evil, are transferred from individual to individual.

Ultimately, all psychologies that are evil will become extinct, and in contrast all psychologies that are good will flourish.

Only the Source and the Mind that is conscious of the Source are eternal as long as humans exist — this form of consciousness is a destiny of humans.

FIFTY ONE

The following is true of most individuals.

One is born into a state of presence in which the essence of all things is simply experienced through presence.

Likewise, an individual is born with an inherent or intuitive desire to explore, learn, and know.

Initially, one has very little ability to distinguish or differentiate aspects of the environment as well as one's emotional reactions to the environment. One's experience is almost entirely of wholeness and the experience of the essence of all things.

Relatively early in one's life, one learns to distinguish and differentiate comfort and discomfort, light and dark, soft and hard.

What was whole and experienced as whole becomes fractured into what seems to be separate essences — but the essence that is of all things is not a physical property, quality, or characteristic bound by physical particulars.

This experience of separation begins one's initiation into participating with countless illusions or forms of unreality.

The most basic distinction one makes early in one's life is pleasurable and not pleasurable. This distinction predates ego, and forms the core of one's psychology — one's individual awakening to opposites of experience as one feels it.

One's primitive psychology begins a process of choice.

Without an ego one simply attempts to move towards the experience of pleasure — discovering and learning in the process who and what creates pleasure and who and what does not.

FIFTY TWO

In the early years of one's life, authorities start the ego-formation process of a child. The ego forms out of an individual's basic personality and psychology in relation to the conditions of the environment.

One of the many functions of the ego is to allow an individual to move through time from one pleasurable experience to another. The ego provides the strength to persevere through periods of discomfort. It maintains in one's body of knowledge a sense of order while experiencing what seems to be disorder. This goes contrary to one's psychology — accepting an experience of discomfort while maintaining the belief or faith that pleasure will return.

The ego separates one from the external and allows one to live in one's imagination, dreams, and thoughts. It is the formation of a core that individuates one from the other, the environment, or the external.

As one's body of knowledge grows, so too does the ego. Strength of the ego allows one to endure longer and more difficult hardships.

The ego's strength grows in relationship to a fundamental distinction: *Does this make me look good in a way that I want or does this make me look bad in a way that I do not want?*

That which causes one to appear good the ego attaches to itself. That which causes one to appear bad the ego distances itself from.

The ego is fundamentally about image and appearances.

In the individuation process the ego eventually becomes a form of one's body of knowledge that seems separate from everything and everyone else.

When the ego individuates to an extreme level of separation, commonly referred to as isolation, often such an individual will experience anhedonia: the inability to experience pleasure or the love of the Source.

If this occurs in the individuation process, it is more than likely that one will experience some form of psychosis.

FIFTY THREE

E very individual is born into a culture that is rooted in a social construct or reality.[28]
Social constructs are based on commonly agreed upon concepts. A few examples of these concepts are:

- Language

- Time

- Distance

- Weight

- Volume

- Monetary Currency

- Authority

- Ownership

A Social Construct creates a social reality. There are five basic social realities:

I. Emergent: A social construct in an early stage of formation.

II. Convergent: An established social construct that is moving towards (Universal Convergent) Reality.

III. Divergent: An established social construct that is moving away from (Universal Convergent) Reality.

IV. Static: A social construct that exists without movement — resulting eventually in stagnation.

V. Universal Convergent: The intersection and unity of all realities existing as one. Experiencing Universal Convergent Reality is to realize Transcendent Consciousness within a society.

FIFTY FOUR

God is one of the greatest concepts and controversies.

Many are willing to die upholding the characteristics and name of their culture's God.

Many cultures believe God is He. Some believe God is She. Other cultures say God is neither, or many, or does not exist.

Cultures attribute many characteristics to God.

Some individuals within cultures claim to personally know or have met God.

Those who believe in God generally believe God to be the highest, the most supreme authority. This authority can be stated as God is *The Good, the Perfect, or the All Knowing*.

Many claim that as humans God is beyond our ability to directly know — *though this does not mean that God does not exist*.

There seems to be built into creation intentions or signs of the direction God guides us to travel in our journey towards the *Good, the Perfect and Knowledge*. The following are a few examples of what has been commonly discovered and accepted as the *right direction* leading towards *these goals or intentions*.

- Peace is better than violence

- Harmony is better than chaos

- Love is better than hate

- Truth is better than lies

- The awareness and knowledge of the health of one's Soul is critical to the health and well-being of everyone

FIFTY FIVE

D ivergent and convergent realities are terms used to describe the direction a society is moving toward in relationship to the Source. Divergent is a society comprised of cultures that are fundamentally moving away from the Source, and convergent is a society comprised of cultures that are fundamentally moving towards the Source.

Universal convergent reality is centered directly in relationship to, and is a full expression of, the Source.

These terms also apply to an individual's direction of change or growth in relationship to the Source.

When an individual's ego ends, perhaps existing only as an echo, the individual begins to experience universal convergent reality. This is to say that the individual becomes increasingly aware of the Source, and as this occurs the individual's awareness of the Mind expands.

In a society or an individual, the expansion of the Mind is a result of the release of stress that happens when the need to support ego ceases and the Source is allowed to flourish.

If an individual enters into universal convergent reality, but the society is divergent, there will be tension between the individual and the society. Likewise, if a society is fundamentally a convergent reality, and an individual is divergent, there will also be tension resulting in stress.

The greatest good emerges when an individual experiencing universal convergent reality is living in a society that is also of this same reality.

When this happens there is the potential for a powerful transformation within the individual as well as the society towards human enlightenment.

FIFTY SIX

The manifestation and expression of Pure Souls is the primary objective of all convergent social realities.

A description of a Pure Soul is best illustrated through the Christian Trinity, which is the Father (Mind), the Son (Source) and the Holy Ghost (The Soul that unites the Mind and Source).

When these three are one in an individual, and unencumbered with the stress of ego, that individual may be said to have a Pure Soul in which the expansion of the Mind becomes infinite, eternal, and whole.

An individual in which such a union occurs is sometimes known as a musician, an artist, a scientist, a writer, and occasionally a prophet, to name just a few social identities.

What differentiates such individuals is not the Source, for the Source is the same in each.

Each individual has a unique body of knowledge and skill through which the Source is able to manifest into existence — into the social reality.

This can be said to be one's primary calling, meaning and purpose, to awaken to and live one's Pure Soul.

FIFTY SEVEN

The following is a primary dilemma of the human condition.

Ego only communicates with ego.

The Source that is one within everyone and everything continuously communicates through the Soul. A fully developed ego that is what the Source is not, has nothing within itself that can identify where the essence of all things comes from, or to even understand the value of the Source beyond simple forms of ego gratification.

The degree to which one relates with ego is the degree to which one's Soul becomes tormented. Because the Soul exists as a channel from the Source to the Mind, when this is blocked or distorted, unconscious as well as conscious confusion occurs or distortion occurs resulting in cognitive dissonance or a psychology in conflict.

The communication from the Source flows though one's body of knowledge. If the communication is directed towards ego, corruption of the truth and reality occurs. If the communication that is pure, as the Source is pure, flows directly into the Mind, purity of Soul occurs.

This is the dilemma — as long as ego exists, corruption and distortion of the essence of all things occurs. Without ego, the essence flows purely into the Mind — resulting in clarity in one's unique expression of the Source.

A Pure Soul living in a culture that allows Pure Souls to exist and express themselves is a life without suffering.

Freedom as a value of a culture is the basic foundation on which such lives are likely to occur. This is the vitality of a culture that is convergent.

FIFTY EIGHT

One's body of knowledge is not ego — though a body of knowledge is the soil from which ego grows.

Likewise, one's body of knowledge is not the Mind — though one is made aware of the Mind through one's body of knowledge.

Ego exists believing that it is the Mind — though it is not.

The Mind is conscious of ego and knows that it is not ego.

Ego frequently believes that it contains and possesses the Source.

The Mind knows that it exists to serve the Source as the Source serves the Mind.

Ego lives in the unreality of imagined future and imagined past.

The Mind lives in the reality of the present.

Ego is mortal and ends with either its disintegration or the death of the body.

The Mind is infinite, eternal, and whole — transcending an individual's life.

Ego exists in time.

Time exists in the Mind only as a concept.

Ego experiences time as a clock.

The Mind experiences time as presence.

One thrives without Ego.

One becomes lost without the Mind.

FIFTY NINE

The core of ego is one's name.

This is one of the primary reasons that monks and nuns receive new names upon initiation into an order of most religions. The intention of receiving a new name is to disconnect one from the ego-orientation of a previous name.

However, shedding one's name does not necessarily mean that the ego is shed.

At the center of one's name or one's ego is "I."

"I" connects the ego with the illusion of self.

"I" separates one's essence from the essence of all things or the Source — differentiating and individuating one's being from other forms of being. This separation is an illusion that is supported by physical properties of time and space.

Without ego "I" is nothing more than a reference to time and space.

Although the Mind, Source, and Soul can be referenced, strictly speaking they cannot be referenced in time and space — they can only be referenced through a state of ongoing experiential knowing.

When one's name and "I" exist for no other purpose than social reference, one exists in a state of knowing through the experience of Soul.

Though there are countless words such as Nirvana, Bliss, Christ Consciousness, and Enlightenment that attempt to describe this state, it is the state of experiential revelation and knowing, and not any particular word or name that is real.

SIXTY

Complete individuation that ends in the disintegration of one's ego is not an easy process, and rarely does it happen quickly.

Drugs can temporarily disintegrate the ego.

Sometimes a tragedy will cause an ego's disintegration.

Some individuals have a powerful epiphany that ends the ego.

However, most contemporary societies encourage and support ego. For youth, it is extremely difficult to function without ego and for most young individuals it is probably counterproductive to the maintenance of one's mental well-being to attempt to exist without ego.

In some areas of work, such as ministry, therapy, and education, it is beneficial to have little or no ego. In most areas of work it is nearly impossible to function without an ego.

However, no matter what one's work is, as one's experiences and studies continue, as one's body of knowledge grows, if one is honest and has integrity in the process of individuation, it will become clear that maintaining the ego causes one to suffer.

Feeding the ego starves the Soul.

Without ego the Soul feeds one's being, one's existence, meaning, and purpose.

A healthy Soul without the burden of ego allows one to come alive.

SIXTY ONE

Temptation is the energy that forms an ego.

Every ego has an origin in an authority that initiates temptation.

Cultures and authorities that serve them are filled with countless temptations.

Temptations exist in the unreality of the future — what *might be* as opposed to what *is*.

What *might be* is culturally defined specifically as a form of success and generally as a form of heaven, a fulfilled life or dream.

Karma is a word that most individuals raised in Western cultures are uncomfortable with. It is a word that sometimes is associated with the concept of *reincarnation*.[29]

Karma that *is not* associated with reincarnation is Pure Soul.

Temptation forms ego. If one pursues a temptation, the ego is fed and in the process one's karma is altered — Pure Soul is corrupted.

This is not to say that a person without an ego does not experience pleasure — it is to say that a person without an ego experiences pleasure as a natural part of life, an experience of the Source, and not as something that alters karma.

Cleaning one's karma is the process of releasing ego, and then the echo of ego, and finally living one's life with a Pure Soul.[30]

SIXTY TWO

When one reaches the end of individuation and begins the process of an ego's disintegration it is not uncommon to experience irrational fears and guilt that are unreal — disconnected from reality.

Doubt is the seed of imagined forms of fear and guilt. It is a culturally created dragon.

The authority of one's ego is the one responsible for the parameters of doubt.

In the beginning, an authority's creation and encouragement of ego is conceived as a form of success. When one individuates and consciously decides to end ego, the psychological inference is failure.

For many individuals, including this author, choosing to release or destroy the ego means journeying through the *Dark Night of the Soul*.

One's ego structure is based on a learned presumption that the authority of one's ego knows who and what to love and not love, and who and what succeeds and fails. In the release of the ego one begins a journey of personally experiencing the counterpart of the ego — those parts of one's being which one presupposed were not worthy of love and which were failures.

At the end of the journey, the dark night, the end of individuation, one's karma is cleaned and one is able to experience the Pure Soul. Doubt diminishes and eventually disappears.

This is awakening to the knowledge of oneself as having always been fully worthy of the love that continuously flows from the Source. It is only the ego, the cultural conditioning that makes one believe otherwise.

This is an experience of heaven and it is infinite, eternal, and whole.

SIXTY THREE

Heaven on earth is not simply possible or hoped for — it is not preventable, though many people attempt to stand in its way.

These people with egos tend to float to the surface of societies. They thrive on fame and publicity. Those without egos tend to live lives of obscurity.

Occasionally a Gandhi, Martin Luther King, or Nelson Mandela, as before mentioned in the endnotes, emerges.

Societies are not unlike the Mind whose purpose is to serve the Source. When the Mind within a social construct recognizes the Source known and expressed in an individual it naturally focuses its attention on serving that individual's life.

This is true in every field of endeavor — of every study.

The healthiest societies are those that are comprised of cultures devoted to the expression of the Source. These societies are convergent realities.

Such societies are those that search for ways to eliminate oppression and containment of the Source.

A society that frees itself from oppression and the related stress that oppression causes is not unlike an individual who is freed from the ego and its related stress.

Every society naturally strives to continue its existence as infinite, eternal, and whole. Free societies are ones in which this has the greatest likelihood of occurring.

SIXTY FOUR

All of creativity flows from the Source into one's body of knowledge.

If the ego directs the creativity, what is created will be something old, copied, duplicated, or repeated. It is like a painter trying to paint the same as another, a writer trying to write what another has written, or a scientist thinking what has already been thought.

When the experience of the Soul directs the creativity, something new and alive will happen.

A society dominated by ego will in time become a static social reality leading eventually to stagnation and ultimately collapse.

A society that invites and encourages Soul is a society that remains vital and alive.

This paradigm is a tension between the new and the old—a condition that humans have always struggled with—fear of the new and complacency with the old.

The Mind whose destiny is to expand understands the old as a foundation from which the new is able to emerge and flourish.

SIXTY FIVE

Like friendship, love, and creativity, consciousness flows from the Source through one's Soul into one's body of knowledge.

The consciousness of ego is a singular perspective.

The consciousness of a Pure Soul is multiple perspectives.[31]

Singular perspective leads to injustice, poverty, and violence.

Multiple perspectives lead to justice, wealth, and peace.

Consciousness through singular perspective leads to imbalance.

Consciousness through multiple perspectives leads to balance.

Singular perspective is exclusive.

Multiple perspectives are inclusive.

A homogenous ecosystem is fragile and least likely to survive.

A heterogeneous ecosystem is vital and most likely to survive.

Individuals with a singular perspective tend towards the early stages of moral development.[32]

Individuals with multiple perspectives tend towards the later stages of moral development.

A Pure Soul's consciousness is universal love and truth.

SIXTY SIX

Equally as important as language, time is a central element or concept of a society, culture, or an individual.

Time exists in all of biological life, if in no other ways than light and dark and climate change associated with seasons.

Humans have discovered numerous ways in which to understand time.

The early ancestors in the Torah were recorded to have lived hundreds of years.[33] However, as many scholars know, when divided by twelve lunar cycles, these ancestors actually lived approximately sixty modern years as calculated by the earth's orbit around the sun.

Understanding and calculation of time has evolved.

There is cosmological time — the time from which the physical universe is believed to have begun.

There is geologic time — transformations on earth covering billions of years.

There are seasonal times in relation to weather associated with the earth's axis in relation to the sun.

There are cultural times related to holidays.

There is basic social time as measured by the clock.

There is time measured by the distance light travels in one second.

Ego understands time in relation to self—one's age in relation to birth and death.

A Pure Soul knows time in relation to infinity, eternity, and wholeness.

A Pure Soul knows that time is an illusion known only by how one measures it.

SIXTY SEVEN

There is another form of time that is referred to here as jungle time.

The contrast of jungle time is human time, which is measured in days, hours, minutes, and seconds.

Jungle time does not have a before or after — it is experienced and known only as presence in relationship to the Source.

Presence is a heightened awareness of what is within oneself and all that is around oneself as experienced within the moment without any forms of separation.

Kurtz, when he is brought out of the jungle, states just before he dies, "the horror."[34]

Departing an eternal state of bliss or presence with the Source, deprived of the possibility of returning, is for the Mind and the Soul of any individual nearly unbearable.

Once one has arrived at nirvana, bliss, or Christ consciousness, the thought of being permanently disconnected from the Source is equivalent to insanity and psychosis.

The Soul cannot survive for long apart from the Source's ocean of love and beauty.

Though human time is necessary and essential to the evolution of civilization, consciousness in jungle time is the experience of infinite perspectives — the destiny of Mind — the Source manifested completely in human form and condition.

SIXTY EIGHT

The original garden spoken about by our ancestors is a state of Mind that exists in time and place recalled as innocence.

In this garden there is a tree of life that is of the Source and there is a tree of the knowledge of good and evil that is of the ego.

At its most developed stage ego is in complete contrast to the Source.

The tree of life is most clearly understood as all of nature and the abundance of all of nature.

Eating of the tree of life is the experience of presence, knowing and the Mind. However, one inevitably experiences pain in such ways as hunger, cold, recalled as innocence. When one experiences pain, one is tempted to eat of the tree of the knowledge of good and evil. Comfort is good and pain is bad. This begins the natural journey of learning to distinguish what causes the first in order to avoid the latter.

Judgments of evil or bad can become very complex. Eventually avoidance of the bad becomes confused and frequently, as a result, avoidance of the good occurs.

The ego's determination of what is bad is sometimes actually what is good.

A Pure Soul living in presence knows only the tree of life. In this, one knows that life is real and good — that which destroys, denigrates, or dismisses the importance of life is not knowledge grounded in what is real and good.

SIXTY NINE

Concepts of masculine and feminine are not of the Source — they are creations of the ego.

When the ego ceases to exist and one awakens fully to the Source, the masculine and feminine attributes that a culture has attached to boy or girl, man or woman, cease to hold meaning.

The pursuit one follows in relation to one's Soul and through one's body of knowledge often has culturally defined qualities as masculine or feminine.

Whether one is anatomically male or female has no applicability to the Source.

Egos often define themselves in a particularly cultured definition of what it means to be masculine or feminine. However, the traits of one's basic personality and psychology antecede cultural definitions.

The English language is an example of a language that does not distinguish between masculine and feminine nouns — does not attribute male or female qualities to anything other than anatomy.

Hard or soft, linear or curved, strong or weak, and firm or gentle are attributes any individual, male or female, can express.

A Pure Soul experiences only the essence of all things without distinction — male or female.

SEVENTY

The greatest illusion perpetrated by almost every culture is the concept of *the end*.

What exist are limitations.

Books have limitations. Movies have limitations. Cultures and knowledge have limitations.

Biological forms have limitations.

We exist in a physical reality of particulars that are limited.

The Mind united with the Source through the Soul is unlimited—though in anything or anyone in particular there is the illusion of having an end.

A book, movie, culture, or knowledge may always be added to.

Biological forms have offspring.

There is no end—there are only forms of continuation.

SEVENTY ONE

Some readers will be aware that the word *spirit* has not yet been discussed.

Many individuals who claim to be *spiritual* and not *religious* seem to be saying that they do not adhere to any dogma, or institutionalized precepts. *Spirit* then becomes many different concepts depending on one's body of knowledge.

Spirit here is the union of love and truth (as stated in this book's introductory remarks). The separation of love and truth is mostly social and cultural — separating feelings from thought. Complete separation of the two is a broken spirit.

Love is generally understood to be a feeling, whereas truth is generally understood to be a thought. However, love is sometimes what one feels and sometimes what one experiences as knowing. Likewise, truth is sometimes what one knows and sometimes what one experiences as feeling.

One experiences the *spiritual* when one experiences love and truth united as one. This experience occurs in many ways such as passion, ecstasy, awe, or inspiration.

Experiencing the *spiritual* is commonly referred to as a state of bliss or grace.

Nature is profoundly influential in revealing *spirit* — so too is a state of communion with others — where the separation of love and truth ceases and one experiences the Source in which they exist as one.

Spirit is a mystical form of energy that one simultaneously knows and feels.

SEVENTY TWO

I t is said that we live *on* the earth and that we live *in* the world.

In the world refers to a collective body of knowledge that an individual connects to with one's own body of knowledge.

Developing one's body of knowledge occurs through one's experience and studies and is extremely important to the health of an individual specifically and to the health of society generally.

It is important that one's body of knowledge emerges or forms from the Source — allowing one to remain connected with the Source as much as possible given one's life circumstances.

A musician's experience and studies are primarily about music. A mathematician's experience and studies are primarily about math. An ornithologist's experience and studies are primarily about birds.

An individual whose Soul is forced to adopt something different than its primary meaning and purpose is an individual who often becomes mentally and emotionally damaged. These individuals will suffer, and will frequently cause others to suffer as well. This is a truth that is firmly planted in the human condition and is not negotiable under any circumstances.

Each individual's Soul is unique. Conformity to something other than what allows the Soul to thrive and give expression is one of the surest recipes for suffering.

It is a Soul's primary purpose to contribute — if blocked or prevented from being allowed to express itself, its reflection will be to destroy rather than create.

SEVENTY THREE

Perfection exists only in and through the Source.
The love that flows through the Source is
perfect love.

In the Source all plurality ends — everything is indistinguishable from everything else.

The essence of all things is perfect.

The Source is like a doorway that leads us to the heaven of God's intention — the Mind free from ego is consciousness of and knowledge of God's intention.

Words and language that are linear and attempt to capture concepts, ideas, and knowledge can never fully or adequately express God's Intention.

The Mind is capable of perceiving multiple concepts, ideas, and knowledge simultaneously — it is in this capability that one is able to comprehend and know God's intention.

Reminders of the Source are also meant to remind one of the purposes of the Source — to facilitate God's intention.

SEVENTY FOUR

There is a story about a great man who most people know.

The great man who had a Pure Soul, so pure, in fact, that the Mind and the Source were indistinguishable. He was in a home in a village with some of his closest friends. They were enjoying one another's company when a loud commotion of anger arose outside. It was as though they were in a boat and a storm had suddenly come upon them.

The disorder of a mob grew louder.

The great man's friends became frightened, but he went to the door and without fear, opened it and walked out amongst the mob and spoke to them.

The shouting and noise subsided. One of his dearest friends came to the door. The great man motioned to his friend to join him. The friend hesitated and then walked out and joined him free of fear.

Overcoming fear is the principal way in which the Mind drawing from the Source is able to expand.

One without fear, like a child, is the infinite, eternal, and whole way in which the Mind experiences itself without limits.

SEVENTY FIVE

The greatest danger for anyone awakening to the Source and the Soul is others who claim to be authorities, particularly close elders, but who are actually thieves.

One's relationship with the Source and Soul is a psychic field that is a psychological temple. It is normal to allow one's elders, particularly those who are actually authorities, entrance into one's temple.

Some elders are undeniably authorities who encourage and nurture one's relationship with the Source. However, some socially designated authority figures are individuals who abuse the sacred entrance into one's temple. Their ego-orientation delights in stealing the dignity and self-respect of others. Their egos grow by consuming others' confidence, maturity, and state of knowing. These individuals are extremely dangerous individuals — often disguised in what a culture teaches is a most trusted form.

Their egos are filled with explanations and justifications for the damage they do.

They normally exist in a present-future unreality — unwilling to examine the events they have created which have caused suffering.

They exist in ego, but not Soul.

They are what were once referred to as demons.

The common contemporary definition of these individuals is *narcissist*.

They are interested only in their personal gratification and survival.

They create divergent social realities in which empathy is not part of their cultures.

SEVENTY SIX

There are aspects of societies that are seductive.

Societies are a mixture of that which seduces the ego and that which honors and directs one's attention to the Source.

Seduction is grounded in the survival instinct — procreation and the avoidance of death. Seduction also arises out of curiosity.

The three most prevalent social seductions are wealth, fame, and titles that hold socially constructed power — they are forms of socially defined status.

If one awakens to the Source, one assumes the difficult undertaking of consciously distinguishing what the social seductions are and the fundamentals of the society that nurture the consciousness of the Source.

The whole of the fundamentals of a society that nurture awareness and knowledge of the Source is the fruit of the Mind blossoming from the Soul.

SEVENTY SEVEN

There are many basic or elementary forms in existence.

There is the point, line, parallel lines, circle, triangle, and square, cross or intersection, oval, sphere, among endless others.

All forms united as one is the Source revealed.

The Source, like the ocean and the sky, has no defense — needs no defense.

The ego's survival is dependent on its defense. Without its defense it disintegrates.

Reality for an enlightened person, an individual with a Pure Soul, is indistinguishable from the person's thought of reality. Thoughts, for an enlightened person, are drawn from the Source, the essence of all things, and are perceived or recognized as form.

Reality and the thought of reality are different for a person with ego. The thought is drawn from the ego's need to be defended — what continues to make the person appear good.

Often a person with ego will believe, state, and defend the position that reality is nothing more than what one chooses to make it.

Those who experience the fullness of the Soul know that reality is not what one makes it, but rather what it is, what has been, and what will always be.

Choosing reality is in reality actually a form of choosing an unreality.

SEVENTY EIGHT

Communication is fundamental to virtually every aspect of the advancement of civilization — individual as well as social.

The most fundamental form of communication is talking, discussion, or dialogue.

Early in one's growth years, talking is a way of learning about the world and oneself and how to interract with the world, which becomes the majority of one's body of knowledge.

Most individuals reach a time in which they believe they have learned about most things and how to do many things.

However, inherent in one's body of knowledge is an ongoing instinctive need to explore. This need to explore eventually leads to a central important human question — *what is love, how do I love and am I loved?*

In its universal form, this question becomes *how does one love, all that is — myself, others, existence, and God?*

This question narrows into one that is very specific — *what and how do I give the best that I have to give in order to express love?*

For each individual, given one's unique body of knowledge, born of highly individualized experiences and studies, the answer is different.

How does the essence of all things flowing through the Soul reveal itself?

This is a fundamental question that a musician, a farmer, a nurse, a builder, a businessman, a writer, an artist, or a statesman must answer.

The answer is revealed without ego.

The correct answer fills the Soul, opens the Mind, and brings about an alleviation of suffering.

SEVENTY NINE

The most expansive and comprehensive reminder of the Source is nature.

Nature does not lie.

An anonymous quote states: *Nothing in living nature happens that is not in relation to the whole.*

Looking out at the mountains, rivers and lakes, the birds and wildlife, the trees and plants one is reminded of the essence of all things: creation.

There is much more that might be written in this book about the Source, the Mind, and the Soul—about the human condition. But the real teacher, the inspiring force of knowledge, is the Source— witnessed in nature and existing in each of us.

The essence of all things is able to become conscious of itself in anyone who is open to its possibility and reality. Although ego plays a part in collective and individual growth and evolution, at some point the ego must end if one is to realize universal consciousness or the Mind.

Many elders who have shed their egos attest to this truth—that although the ego is useful for playing many types, and levels of games, it serves little meaning and purpose for a Soul longing to awaken to the inspiration and beauty of the Source.

POSTLUDE

Home

After many days journeying I arrived on the hillside over-
looking the village of my people.

I sat down in the tall grass and looked out over my
home. I watched the people go about their daily business.

They are a village of fishermen — the homes nestled
around a cove from which each day they sail.

They are not yet time travelers — still being content
with the way things are.

I pondered how far we have come, while aware that in
spite of what any of us might believe, we have really just
begun.

What we will learn is anyone's guess. Mysteries about
life have no end.

We are a convergent social reality.

We want to know the truth — to overcome our superstitions and fears — to feel at peace and one with all that
is — the essence of all things.

As I watch my people walk about the village, I observe
a stranger walking along the sands from the south. I am

aware that he is a hunter. And although I am at quite a distance, I can see that he carries with him a leather pouch.

I rise, knowing it is time for me to rejoin my family and friends.

It is time for me, along with the village elders, to greet the stranger.

THE SOUND OF WATER

Several years ago I was a member of a taskforce that was
a part of a state mental health law reform commission. I
attended a conference that was held at a beautiful, large,
but not extravagant hotel.

I woke the first morning of the conference, ate break-
fast, and walked to the conference center next to the
hotel.

The conference room was large, easily capable of seat-
ing three or four hundred people. As I entered, I noticed
how dark the room was, how distant the seats of taskforce
members were from the Commissioners' seats near the
front. On the left of the stage area, next to the moderators'
table was a large screen that was used for slides of data,
and PowerPoint presentations. Sitting in the conference
room felt very much like Plato's famous metaphor of life
and learning as beginning in a cave on which one can only
see shadows.

I sat through several hours, listening to the drone
of information and opinions. I decided to go outside,
to take a break from what seemed very much like a lot
of noise.

The weather was comfortable, neither too hot nor too cold, and the sky was clear and blue. It was a very beautiful day.

Although there were a few occasional joggers and pedestrians, standing outside I felt a sense of quiet peaceful solitude in which my Mind silenced and opened.

It was then that I heard the fountain I was standing next to. It was quite elaborate with a multitude of steps over which the water flowed. I heard the sound of the water and was immediately brought into the present, away from the conference room.

I became mesmerized, entranced by the water's sound. It was as though it spoke, telling stories distant and present, fictional and real.

The sound spoke of farmers throughout the ages who when experiencing a drought became anxious waiting day after day for the sound of water and then becoming overjoyed when they heard the sound of rain.

The sound spoke of those who traveled long distances through deserts and wastelands with lips parched and bodies thirsty, who suddenly heard the sound of a stream, a river, or falls. The sound spoke of life's beginning and life's renewal.

The sound of the water I heard from the fountain that day was a soft voice whispering the sound of the Soul of the listener listening.

ONTOLOGICAL
FIELD THEORY

Cosmological

$e = mc^2$ Where: e is "energy"

m is "mass"

c is "speed of light" (186,000 miles/second)

Ontological

$e = kp_2^2$ Where: e is "enlightenment" defined as energy in the form of consciousness.

$k\,(p_1)$ is "knowing" or "knowledge" defined as the sum of connectedness and relatedness commonly referred to as "wholeness."

p_2 is "presence" defined as the sum of all physical laws occurring simultaneously within one's purview.

When "mass" collapses (creating a "black hole"), at the moment of complete collapse, the transition point, $e=mc^2$ becomes:

$$e \mathbin{\#} mc^2$$

When "knowledge" or "knowing" collapses (creating a "pinpoint" of perspective $[p_1]$), at the moment of complete collapse, the transition point, $e=kp_2^2$ becomes:

$$e \mathrel{\#} kp_2^2$$

In both instances of "collapse," superposition happens — the "event" simultaneously exists as "equal to" and "not equal to." In this "moment," the *Ontological Field Equation* exists as:

$mc^2 \mathrel{\#} e \mathrel{\#} kp_2^2$ and can be written either as $e \mathrel{\#} mc^2$ or $e \mathrel{\#} kp_2^2$ depending from which direction one approaches the moment of "collapse."

This moment can be graphed as:

$$e = kp_2^2 \qquad\qquad mc^2 \mathrel{\#} e \mathrel{\#} kp_2^2 \qquad\qquad e = mc^2$$

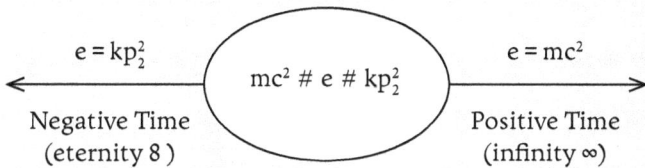

Negative Time (eternity 8) ← → Positive Time (infinity ∞)

(Note: "Negative" does not mean backward, and "Positive" does not mean forward. They are opposite directions away from the Source)

ONTOLOGICAL FIELD THEORY

(Sides to the Equation)

$e=mc^2$	$e=kp_2^2$
Left Hemisphere	Right Hemisphere
Invasive Culture	Native Culture
Time = Clock = Human Time	Time = Presence = Jungle Time
Linearity	Wholeness
Infinity	Eternity
Beginning and End are Differentiated	Beginning and End are Undifferentiated
Exclusive	Inclusive
Primarily Intellectual	Primarily Intuitive
Mathematical Equations	Artistic Equations
Conditional Love	Unconditional Love
Unconscious is unknown	Unconscious is known
"Spirit" is Noun	"Spirit" is Verb
Ownership is Maximized	Ownership is Minimized
"Beauty" can be Possessed	"Beauty" cannot be Possessed
Aging is not Respected	Aging is Respected
Sequence is important	Connectedness is important
Positive (+) time exists	Negative (-) time exists
Infinity sign: ∞	Eternity sign: 8
Present with future is dominant	Present with past is dominant
Social reality unifies	Conscious reality unifies
Closed Mind	Open Mind
Emphasis on subjective	Emphasis on objective
God is written in a Book	God is written in the Environment

Collapse of One's Body of Knowledge

1. The ego creates a body of knowledge.

2. When one experiences the essence of all things conscious of itself in one's being the ego collapses, disintegrates, or is in some form destroyed.

3. One's body of knowledge collapses around the Source.

4. One's perspective is released from the ego and enters the Mind.

5. The Source and the Mind are united.

6. This union becomes a Pure Soul.

7. One awakens to the realization that the body of knowledge is not one's own — it is of the collective conscious and Mind.

EPILOGUE

Earth is one of the rarest of planets.

Humans are the rarest of species.

Humans are conscious of the concept of death and survival.

Humans have an unlimited ability to unravel mystery.

It is not possible for any individual to survive in body.

It is possible, though not certain, that humans may survive forever.

This is the goal of the Pure Soul.

ENDNOTES

1. A creator of superstitions and false beliefs can be male or female or both.
2. From John 4, New International Version of the Bible.
3. Developed egos frequently form into an archetype. Throughout *The Sound of Water* ego and archetype are often synonymous.
4. In *The Sound of Water* the Source is understood through the life of the Second Person of the Christian Trinity — the Son of the Heavenly Father — Jesus Christ.
5. In *The Sound of Water* the Soul is understood to be the Third Person of the Christian Trinity — The Holy Spirit or the Holy Ghost.
6. David Koresh, Jim Jones, and Adolph Hitler are examples.
7. Examples of particulars are fame, status, wealth, or power. They are particulars when they exist as goals one strives to achieve, and not the natural result of living one's life correctly in relation to the Source.
8. The field of consciousness, or the kingdom of heaven on earth, is composed of the multitude of individuals who are without egos. The *ego* is the seed of separation. A human cannot become a conscious adult without first developing and then dissolving and transcending an ego. During one's early years one needs to identify and individuate. This process is the development of an ego

called "*I.*" An ego allows an individual to separate, distinguish and comprehend components of various realities. However, the development of the ego also has the effect of creating isolation which in a myriad of ways has the potential of causing psychological and sociological discord.

9. Although it is written: *In the beginning was the Word, and the Word was with God, and the Word was God* (John 1:1), it is the meaning without words that the Word is meant to awaken.

10. *Belonging* is a human concept. There is no way of knowing whether it is an applicable concept that applies to God.

11. The proper object of the human intellect is reality; all true knowledge is knowledge of reality. Reality of itself is manifestly knowable, intelligible, and thus potentially or fundamentally true; and, on the other hand, intellect is, according to the measure of its capacity, a faculty of insight into all reality, into whatever is real; *intellectus potens fieri omnia; anima...quodammodo fit omnia.* Deny either of these postulates regarding the terms of the ontological relation, reality and Mind, and all rational thought is instantly paralyzed. Hence, in so far as a reality becomes an actual object of human knowledge it has formal ontological truth in relation both to the human Mind and to the Divine Mind; while antecedently to human thought it is fundamentally true, or intelligible, to the human Mind, and of course formally true in relation to the Divine Mind. (Peter Coffey, *Ontology or the Theory of Being*)

12. Some readers may prefer the word *transforming*.

13. This process is true for many different professions such as an artist, a mathematician, a gardener, a theologian, and so forth.

14. W. Windelband, *A History of Philosophy*, The Macmillon Company, 1905

15. An example of a title is lawyer, doctor, or professor. A lifetime of practicing these professions is very different than what one imagines that the title implies.

16. Some psychologists, therapists, and counselors think of the unconscious as other-worldly forms of existence — as though the collective unconscious emanates out of some mysterious realm into our dreams, thoughts, and behaviors, and that the totality of every individual's unconscious is some sort of surreal cloud called the "collective unconscious." This other-worldly interpretation of the unconscious is incorrect. During the early years of each of our lives, our brains are forming neural connections as we experience the environment around us, and the reactions within us. Our brains at this time have little if any information that allows us to process what we are experiencing. Not only do we not have language, we have no knowledge of "sequence," "cause and effect," or "time." In short, the world around us, and in us, is processed as "random." Eventually we learn that the light in the room comes on when someone flips a switch allowing electricity to move through a wire that enters the bulb resulting in a physical event that produces light. Eventually we learn that a person does not change colors. We learn that a person has changed their shirt. A person does not disappear. A person leaves the room. In other words, during our early years when our brain is first forming connections, information is stored and comprehended in quite random ways. This early period is also a time when "universal" experiences occur. Every child knows hunger, warmth, comfort, feeling tired, feeling alert, love, fear, frustration, and so on. This is the

time in one's life, when the seemingly random nature of the environment, and the very real feelings associated with living are stored in the brain, without socially constructed filters. This early formation of the brain is what constitutes the "individual" as well as the "collective" unconscious or memories that are universal to the human experience. Additionally, geometric shapes, colors and sounds are internalized before definition and explanation are established. These become symbols that are universal, and arise in almost every time and place — every culture. Once one begins to learn language, sequence, cause and effect, as well as time, one's consciousness begins to form, and one's "ego" or "narrative" begins, separating one's self from unconscious knowledge and perception.

17. A developed counterpart to one's ego becomes, in Jungian terminology, one's shadow.

18. Examples of reminders are churches, rituals, Holy Scriptures and iconic sounds and symbols.

19. There are many ways and many verbs to describe the cessation of an ego. The experience is unique to every individual.

20. Matthew 18:3, New International Version of the Bible.

21. Saint John of the Cross

22. T.S. Eliot, *Here is no water but only rock,* Harcourt, Brace and World, Inc., 1952

23. Dr. Martin Luther King Jr., Mahatma Gandhi, and Nelson Mandela, to name just a few, are examples of such individuals.

24. New International Version of the Bible: John 14:6 Jesus answered, "I am the way and the truth and the life. No one comes to the Father except through me."

25. Anonymous quote.

26. Examples of dragons are time, holidays, and the American dream.

27. G. Spencer-Brown, *Laws of Form*, E.P. Dutton, a Division of Elsevier-Dutton Publishing Co., Inc., 1979

28. A Social Construct is any group of two or more individuals. In the smallest of ways it is a mother and a son or daughter, a father and a son or daughter, a wife and a husband, a brother and a sister or a couple. It is a family, a neighborhood, a church, a school, an organization, agency, workplace, or ultimately the collective body of humanity. A Social Construct has values, reward systems, psychology, expectations, opportunities, in essence a *social narrative*.

29. Reincarnation is speculation that many philosophers and theologians question its validity.

30. This process in Western cultures is commonly referred to as *putting one's house in order*.

31. The Christian Trinity, when united with *Perspective*, produces a Quaternity of wholeness.

32. Kohlberg's *Stages of Moral Development*

33. Genesis: Chapter 5

34. J. Conrad, *Heart of Darkness*, Random House, 1993

ABOUT THE AUTHOR

Joshua K. Linden grew up in the Midwest. After working for several years in California, he moved to Virginia where he completed his education with a degree in counseling.

He is married and lives in the countryside of Central Virginia with his wife and two dogs.

In addition to writing, he continues his love of ceramics, painting, and music — drawing inspiration from nature.

The Sound of Water is a culmination of seven years of reflection on the state of the human Soul.

Visit Joshua online at: *www.joshuaklinden.com*

www.ingramcontent.com/pod-product-compliance
Lightning Source LLC
Chambersburg PA
CBHW031207270326
41931CB00006B/453